Presented To:

_____

By: _____

Date: _____

Do you desire the wisdom of Solomon?

The courage of Deborah?

The boldness of Peter?

Perhaps the loyalty of Ruth?

Life's Little Handbook of Wisdom II contains over 500 winning ways to live your life according to biblical and everyday wisdom. . .and become the person you've always desired!

LIFE'S
LITTLE HANDBOOK
OF WISDOM

Volume Two

Bruce and Cheryl Bickel
Stan and Karin Jantz

A BARBOUR BOOK

Published by **Barbour and Company, Inc.**
P.O. Box 719
Uhrichsville, Ohio 44683

ISBN 1-55748-644-1

Printed in the United States of America

A knot never unties itself.

Spend your time talking *to* someone instead of *about* them.

Fear diminishes incentive, but courage increases productivity.

Accept your children for who they are,
not what you want them to be.

Men: When you get a haircut, get them
all cut.

Satan certainly knows the value of
time. When you feel overwhelmed,
remember this.

Loving your spouse is not enough.
Learn how to demonstrate your love.

Be generous with praise and stingy with criticism.

Move from involvement to commitment.

▬▬▬

If you lose money on every deal, you can't make it up in volume.

Budget for a future. Don't outlive your money.

Own a really good set of yard tools, or find a neighbor who does (and borrow them occasionally).

You can't plan for the future by looking in the rearview mirror.

Certain circumstances are simply the result of our bad choices, not the work of Satan.

Live somewhere between complacency and crisis.

LIFE'S
LITTLE HANDBOOK
OF WISDOM

In matters of style, go with the flow; in matters of conscience, stand firm.

Get off the bus two stops early and walk to your destination.

Lust and love may feel the same, but lust always takes and love always gives.

Your boss will be more impressed by what you finish than by what you attempt.

Initiative is seeing what needs to be done and doing it before you are asked.

No one will ever accuse you of being a boring conversationalist if you let people talk about themselves.

Avoid cars with flat tires and friends with big egos. Both require constant pumping.

A Bible on the shelf is worthless; a Bible being read is priceless.

Always be at least as courteous to members of your family as you are to strangers.

Don't stick out your chest when
someone pats you on the back.

There are a few nuts (and squirrels) in
every family tree.

You will learn more from adversity than
from prosperity.

LIFE'S
LITTLE HANDBOOK
OF WISDOM

A vacation is more enjoyable if you stay within your budget.

When it comes to eternity, seats are available in the smoking and the nonsmoking sections. What is your pleasure?

Here's how to make Sunday worship more meaningful: Think of yourself as a participant rather than a spectator.

Try to avoid a long face and a narrow mind.

Others determine your reputation. You determine your character.

Don't take pride in exceeding your expectations if your goals were only mediocre.

Defending your Christian faith will not be a problem if your faith is not noticeable.

Christmas gifts should be filled with love, not expectations.

When opportunity knocks, don't
complain about the pounding.

Give your time, not excuses.

A true sense of humor does not rely on
the humiliation of others.

LIFE'S
LITTLE HANDBOOK
OF WISDOM

———

A good life is of more value than a good living.

Laugh at yourself as much as others do

Resist the temptation to misrepresent the merchandise. That includes yourself.

Making a mistake is forgivable, but
repeating it is not.

The time to worry about your money is
before you spend it.

Some friendships, unlike marriages,
work better long distance.

Planning how to get money without
earning it is a futile exercise.

Try to read the handwriting on the wall
before your back is up against it.

Don't be obsessed with losing weight.
Rearranging those pounds doesn't
sound so bad.

You may have to light a fire under some people to get them going. For others, dynamite may be the answer.

Anticipate the unexpected.

You will be holier if you give yourself wholly to God.

The secret behind most success stories?
One word: drive.

Wisdom is not inherited, except from
your Heavenly Father.

If you have a high opinion of yourself,
keep it a secret.

You know you have a good sense of
humor if you can laugh when someone
tells your joke better than you.

Pride in yourself is like a slip. You
shouldn't let it show.

What you think about when you have
nothing to do reveals what is important
to you.

God speaks. Do you listen?
God commands. Do you obey?
God leads. Do you follow?

Ignore a strong opinion that is without
conviction.

There is little benefit to acquiring
wealth if you fail at managing it.

Have a sharp mind, keen wit, and discriminating tongue.

Some good deeds should be remembered and some forgotten. Remember those done by others; forget your own.

You aren't living within your means if you have to borrow money to do it.

LIFE'S
LITTLE HANDBOOK
OF WISDOM

Everyone in heaven will be an
immigrant, but there will be no
temporary visas.

Use your influence sparingly. It will
last longer.

Don't overlook life's simple pleasures.
Appreciate scratching an itch.

Discover what pleases God, and then make them habits.

Principles last longer than popularity.

You can't stand against Satan if you don't kneel before God.

LIFE'S
LITTLE HANDBOOK
OF WISDOM

An open mind and a closed mouth are
better than the opposite.

A smile is your most important
accessory.

No one knows he is fortunate until he is
unfortunate.

A bald head is nothing to be ashamed of if one wears it well. (Put a feather in your cap!)

Failure is the end only if you stop trying.

You are as big as the things that annoy you.

Display what you believe by how you behave.

Hindsight is good; foresight is better; insight is best.

Wealth can be inherited, but esteem must be earned.

Ambition without ability is useless;
ability without ambition is wasted.

Live longer by worrying less.

Make sure your uniqueness draws
people to you, not drives them away.

▬▬

Appreciate differences instead of criticizing them.

Men and women, regardless of age, share these common needs: trust, acceptance, appreciation, and love.

If you prepare for the future, you won't have to worry about it.

It is easier to change your behavior in advance than to change your reputation afterward.

If you look at others *with* love, you won't have to look at others *for* love.

Every morning you choose your attitude for the day.

Procrastinating on a decision may be a decision in itself.

Clip a cartoon and send it to a friend.

If you tell your spouse of your love often enough, you'll never have to ask if your spouse loves you.

Compliments pave the way to a smile, a handshake, or a kiss.

Pick a favorite color other than beige.

No one regrets at life's end that they spent too much time with their children.

LIFE'S
LITTLE HANDBOOK
OF WISDOM

———

Accept the possibility that most people won't have the insight to realize how great you really are.

Be more curious about ideas than you are about your neighbors.

Practice good dental hygiene.

Respect the power of love. Abhor the love of power.

Indifferent people never make a difference.

What happens to you may be an accident. How you respond is not.

Enjoy the detour.

A good example is better than good advice.

Be more concerned with the heritage you'll leave to your children than the inheritance you'll receive from your parents.

A pleasant expression increases your face value.

Don't pray for a lighter load; pray for a stronger back.

You show what you are by what you laugh at.

LIFE'S
LITTLE HANDBOOK
OF WISDOM

■■■■■■

Your dreams won't come true if you're
sleeping.

You can't shake hands with a clenched
fist.

Think twice before you ask your boss to
pay you what you're worth.

"Large portions" is not necessarily a glowing recommendation for a restaurant.

Popularity usually isn't worth the sacrifice.

The man who takes inordinate praise is not worthy of it.

Make at least one person smile, at least once a day.

A stupid question is less embarrassing than a stupid mistake.

You can't put your foot in your mouth if your lips are closed.

If your prayers don't mean anything to you, they mean even less to God.

Sometimes you say more by speaking less.

Distinguish between opportunity and temptation.

Truth is not determined by how many people believe it.

Moments are the pearls in the string of a lifetime.

If you can laugh at yourself, you are guaranteed a lifetime of chuckling.

There are many things in life you cannot change. Your attitude is not one of them.

Profanity is nothing more than the display of a stunted vocabulary.

A thick skin and a short memory are the best weapons against unjust criticism.

Conduct yourself as if Christ is watching you. He is.

Too many advantages for your children add up to a disadvantage.

If you're too busy to laugh, you're too busy.

Rest on God's promises; stand behind
yours.

Be kind to unkind people. It kind of
gets 'em.

Kiss your kids goodnight every evening,
even if it wakes them up.

Being a good example is better than
giving good advice.

The kind of friends you can buy aren't
worth the price you pay.

Examine your own life for the faults you
find most irritating in others.

Learn to have a good time without spending a lot of money.

Courage is not the absence of fear; it is the ability to act in the presence of fear.

God wants coordinated Christians. He wants their walk to match their talk.

■■■■■

Know the difference between tolerance
and permissiveness.

Speak *with* your children, not *at* them.
Sit *with* your children, not *on* them.

If you can't get to sleep for one night,
check your pillow.
If you can't get to sleep for two nights,
check your mattress.
If you can't get to sleep for three nights,
check your conscience.

A good sermon is determined more by
the listener's response than by the
preacher's speech.

We love God because we know who He
is. God loves us despite who we are.

Remember the punchline *before* you tell
the joke.

LIFE'S
LITTLE HANDBOOK
OF WISDOM

———

A short temper can be dispelled by
longer prayers.

Ask questions.

Remember *when* you got married.
Remember *where* you got married.
Remember *why* you got married.

Choose fashion over fads.

You can tell volumes about where you're going by remembering where you've been.

Don't worry about what you can't do. If you must worry, worry about why you won't do what you should do.

In matters of principle, don't give in and don't give up.

Celebrate your spouse's birthday, but hold the relish to tell jokes about age.

You can tell a little about a person by his opinion of himself. You can tell a lot about a person by what others say about him. You can tell even more by what he says about others.

You should have an open mind, not an empty one.

There is a difference between being a gossip and being informative.

If you don't stand for anything, you may fall for everything.

Welcome the friend who speaks harshly about you to your face.

Approach life's adversities with an attitude that makes you better, not bitter.

Your dreams won't come true if you allow them to languish.

Don't leave the sermon at the church.

Don't run with the ball unless you know the direction of the goal.

The times when you need God the most are when you don't think you need Him.

Acquire good ideas; abandon bad habits.

You are less likely to fall into temptation if you don't walk along the edge.

A small kindness expressed today is better than a grand intention planned for tomorrow.

Let money be your servant, not your master.

Just because it is in print does not make it worth reading. Just because it is on TV does not make it worth watching.

Avoid being long in the face or round in the stomach.

When you are putting out a fire, don't argue about changing the nozzle on the hose.

You can't get ahead by trying to get even.

Success is a matter of luck only for those who never succeed.

Delayed obedience is disobedience.

Prayer without effort will be insincere.
Effort without prayer will be ineffective.

Don't mistake attraction for love.

Encouragement, praise, and recognition are often more effective than a raise or bonus, and they are always cheaper.

It is better to be the one who get things done than the one who gets the credit.

Decorate your home with hospitality.

Your most valuable asset could be your character. Unfortunately, it can't be used as collateral for a loan.

The Christian life should be based more on faith than on feelings.

If you start the day with the expectation that nothing meaningful will occur, you will probably get what you expect.

——

Deal creatively with adversity. When
you can't pay the electric bill, have a
romantic dinner by candlelight.

Criticism and success are both difficult
to handle, but one is ultimately more
enjoyable.

A person becomes an antique when she
collects dust instead of contributes.

66

Vary your routines so they do not become ruts.

Do more than you are asked to do, and more than what is expected.

You won't like the harvest if you have sown seeds of bitterness.

■■■■■

There is only one difference between the person who completes a marathon and the person who doesn't. The finisher didn't give up when he wanted to.

Don't confuse activity with results.

Prefer the love of your family over the praise of acquaintances.

Live what the Bible teaches. Don't merely quote Scripture.

Anxiety is shortlived if we give it to God.

Optimism must have some basis in fact, or it is merely fantasy.

Not everyone who survives the battle
deserves to be a general.

Seek to know God and faith will follow.

Mental attitude is often more important
than mental capacity.

The generous man always has more than he needs; the greedy man never has enough.

Do something now that will be a pleasant memory later.

Maybe Peter couldn't walk on the water, but at least he got out of the boat.

Appreciate simplicity.

Cherish tranquility.

Teach your children by your words
(make sure they are kind); by your
actions (make sure they are
wholesome); and by your temperament
(make sure it is controlled).

Don't stay committed to a set of plans that is not working.

An exceptional leader is one who gets average people to do superior work.

Gossip should never be disguised as concern.

True faith involves doing all you can
and letting God take care of the rest.

Do it today.

A marriage can be a great investment
that yields tremendous dividends, if you
have the interest.

Some of your best thinking can take place in the shower. (And a steamy shower door makes an excellent notepad.)

Difficulties are opportunities for growth. If you try to avoid all trials, you are simply arresting your development.

LIFE'S
LITTLE HANDBOOK
OF WISDOM

If you think you are humble, you are mistaken.

Discord precedes deterioration.

Don't tease the dog unless you're sure he can't jump over the fence.

Dare to be yourself.

If you try to please everybody, nobody will like you.

The measure of your success is not what is in your wallet but what is in your heart.

When you play a team for the third time
that you defeated twice before, be careful.

Arguing with the umpire will not
change the call. However, you'll be
allowed to display your conviction.

Convert your failures into successes by
learning from them.

Don't wait to do one *great* thing for the Lord in your lifetime. Rather, many good *little* things accomplished for the sake of His kingdom is in itself a great thing.

Try to make a good impression on more than just your pillow.

■■■■■■■■

Principles are not determined by majority vote.

Your future is not confined to the circumstances of the present.

Bad habits you fail to control will eventually control you.

If you're careful in choosing your friends, you won't have to waste time changing them.

Seeing is better than looking.
Listening is better than hearing.
Doing is better than talking.

The righteous woman of God may be called to stand with an unpopular minority.

God doesn't promise you a life without difficulties. But He does promise that He will always be with you.

A signpost, like a peer, only warns you about the road ahead. But a map, like a mentor, can show you how to get where you want to go.

Let your primary motivation be the still small voice of the Holy Spirit.

Give an excuse only if you would accept it from someone else.
Truth is not defined by popularity.

Motivation increases when we assume large responsibilities with a short deadline.

Choices determine consequences.

If you look for the best in people, you are likely to find value in everyone.

Don't let adverse circumstances change your faith. Have faith that God can change your circumstances.

Don't be content with a mediocre
performance if you can do better.

Much of the criticism we receive may be
unjust, but probably some of it is valid.

You will attract people who are like
yourself.

■■■■■

Enthusiasm is the antidote to boredom.

The salesperson who uses pressure to close the sale either has poor technique or questionable merchandise.

You won't win the race if you don't leave the starting block.

People are more likely to do that which they believe to be to their own advantage.

Listening to gossip is as wrong as spreading it.

Two-faced people can't put their best face forward.

If God has not called you to be a church leader, be careful how you criticize those who are.

To get out of the dark, turn on the lights.

Sometimes, for the sake of your faith, disagree with those who disagree with you.

No one does the right thing naturally.
It takes effort and practice.

The only thing worse than thinking
you're a big shot is acting like one.

Every time you read a book by a new
author, go back and read a classic that
has stood the test of time.

It is true that Christianity is good.
More important, Christianity is true.

It's easy to be a good neighbor when a
neighbor is in trouble. Try being a good
neighbor all the time.

God's plans are always perfect. That
said, seek His will.

If you believe for a moment that you own even a single possession, your contentment will be tied to it.

Know your strengths and weaknesses; interests and passions; and gifts and skills.

The way you think about God does not define Him.

91

Ego can be summarized in three words: power, position, and prestige.

You can start your day without God, but you'll never really get started.

Here's a tip for the next time you write one of those Christmas letters nobody reads: Make up a bunch of stuff and see if anybody calls.

Pursue personal holiness at all costs.

Feeling good about God does not bring you closer to Him.

One time in your life, leave home on a vacation without any idea what you are going to do or where you are going to go.

Here's a fashion tip: Buy everything a size bigger than what you think you need. People will think you're losing weight.

If you want to know God's will, spend time with Him.

Knowing God takes tremendous effort, but the reward is great.

Romance may begin with a foot rub.

A friend is one whose strengths
complement your weaknesses.

Some enjoy the solitude of the early
morning, while others appreciate the
quietude of blackest night. Most of us
struggle with the time in between.

The Bible says that the eyes of the Lord roam the earth looking for people whose hearts are completely His. Guess what? He's still looking.

Next time you read a really great book, make every effort to get in touch with the author.

The same thing applies to the Bible.

The earth is God's creation, not mother nature's.

The media are in the business of entertainment. True enlightenment may be found elsewhere.

Think of your net worth as what you have given rather than what you have.

Consider how you can make a bigger impact with your time, money, and talents.

Ignore something bad if ignoring it makes it go away.

God knows what's in our hearts. We might as well get right to the point.

The more specific you make your giving,
the more likely you will effect change.

If you hire someone to do something you
could do if you had the time, make sure
you spend the time you have wisely.

Activities that are good for you may be tough in the short term but rewarding in the long term.

If you can't live without it, go home and sleep on it.

Before you financially support an individual or an organization, find out if the following characteristics are evident: purpose, strategy, and accountability.

If a writer makes you mad, find out if he's telling the truth. Like the course of a debilitating virus, the subtle propagation of falsehoods may be devastating.

Don't throw money at problems.

When you pray, be careful to
distinguish your needs from your
desires.

None of us gets everything we ask for,
nor should we.

A bad habit is like a leaky faucet. The longer you let it go, the worse it gets.

Give money to people or organizations you can stay personally involved with.

If you leave the car on E(mpty), tell the next d(river).

You usually lose interest in something that's out of focus.

Your needs will always outweigh your energy.

Establish family traditions and faithfully keep them.

Exposing yourself to God's truth is risky, but it's a risk worth taking.

Power begins to corrupt the moment you begin to seek it.

The essence of Christianity is new life in Christ. The essence of Christ is victory over death.

Morality must always take a back seat
to holiness. One is the driver, the other
the passenger.

About the only things you can control
are the choices you make.

Just say no. Addictions to urgency,
mediocrity, and procrastination are
painful habits to kick.

Empowering is more effective than delegating.

The next time you feel weak in the knees, try using them to pray.

Giving is more fulfilling when you align it with your interests and goals.

God created us and Jesus saved us. All
we must do is believe.

Always hold the view that your most
productive years are ahead of you.

Your best friends will criticize you
privately and encourage you publicly.

Change is a process, not an event.

If you ever get the thought that computers will replace books, try curling up in your favorite chair with a PC.

You will never be humble before God if you think He needs you.

Even if you're walking side by side, you can communicate face to face.

One can start something and never begin it.

Managing the events in our lives can be made easier by managing the transitions between them.

Ask your kids to name their heroes.
You'll probably be surprised.

Encourage your children's interest in
positive role models.

Spend time with your kids now, and
they'll spend time with you later.

Pray with your kids. Every day.

Find reasons to celebrate your family.

Be the first to throw old underwear
away.

Prepare breakfast for your family on
Sunday morning.

A spiritually mature individual places
more importance on God's internal
presence than on the world's external
signs.

LIFE'S
LITTLE HANDBOOK
OF WISDOM

Make a date to go out to dinner with
your spouse at least once a month.
Showing genuine appreciation is an art.

Thoughtful compliments wear better
than impulsive flattery.

Don't miss these "firsts" in your child's life: the first word spoken; the first steps taken; the first day of school; the first graduation; the first game won; the first game lost; the first big heartbreak; the first big success.

When exercise becomes as natural as eating, you will begin to eat more naturally.

Try doing without TV for a week.

Action usually precedes attitude.

Place fresh flowers in the places where you live and work.

Discipline is at the heart of discipleship.

Prayer involves listening to God as well as speaking to Him.

Remember that a handwritten note beats a typed one every time.

LIFE'S
LITTLE HANDBOOK
OF WISDOM

Keep a notepad in your Bible.

Buy a book of blank pages and keep a
journal. Record your spiritual and
personal thoughts and feelings daily,
even if you only write a couple of
sentences.

To earn someone's trust, pay them first some respect.

An appropriate touch can be an effective healer.

Engage yourself in a ministry and be able to articulate your purpose in one sentence.

119

Energize, empower, and equip the people who look to you for leadership.

Do your best to return phone calls the day you receive them.

Help the helpless and give to the needy, but do it out of compassion, not pity.

Passion and compassion are closely related.

Strive to have a Christian lifestyle.

You tend to have a greater sense of purpose when, for one thing, you believe God made you.

Be teachable every day.

Provide a forum where the people who look to you for leadership can express their feelings and ideas without fear of reprisal.

Shelves filled with books are like a beckoning lighthouse in a cloak of fog.

Build your personal library with hard-cover books that will transcend centuries and circumstances.

Reading books on a variety of subjects broadens your personal knowledge and appeal.

Pay attention to the design of the things you buy, and then buy the things with the best design.

In general, spend twice as much but buy half as many.

Get into the habit of writing thank-you notes, even for little things or acts of kindness.

Try to empower, rather than control, anyone who looks to you for leadership.

Get a concordance and look up the
names of God.

Force yourself to read poetry; start with
the Psalms.

Teach children in some way throughout
your life.

Set aside a designated period of time each day, each week, each month, and each year to focus on God.

Forgiveness is at the heart of love.

Be involved in the results of commerce, not ground up in its wheels.

One of the sobering characteristics of leadership is that leaders are judged to a greater degree than followers.

Since exhaustion begins and ends on the inside, that's where genuine rest must originate.

Filling an existing need can be as valuable as anticipating a new one.

127

It's a joy to steer heavenward someone who's been going south.

Next time you pack a suitcase, take an inner journey to see where you are.

Never lose sight of the mysteries of life.

Sometimes what you don't know is more intriguing than what you know.

The moment you regret something you've said, make plans to deliver an apology.

Have the courage to hold people accountable.

Managing people begins with caring for them.

Rather than using God to solve your problems, use your problems to get close to God.

Create a balance in your life between being a spectator and a participant.

A road map isn't much good if you don't know where you're going.

It's one thing to *know* what's right, and another thing entirely to *do* it.

When you talk to children, get to their level and look them in the eye.

■■■■■

There are many areas in life that require constant maintenance: your yard, your garage, your house, your relationships.

A wink delivers a powerful message, so be careful to whom you send it.

When establishing rules, make as few as possible and enforce them as consistently as you can.

Time cannot be controlled. You can only control yourself.

Whenever you look back at your life, be positive.

Whenever you look at the present, be realistic.

Whenever you look to the future, be bold.

It's a good thing to delight in the Lord, but how much better when the Lord delights in you.

There is a direct relationship between the desire to know God and the struggle that follows.

134

Rather than worry about what you don't know about God, concentrate on what you know.

Get a concordance and study the names of Jesus.

You can't network, strong-arm, or kick-back your way into heaven. Your faith is worth the price of admission.

━━━━

Whenever you're tempted to go with the grain, consider going against it.

Tell your kids they have a special future and then do all you can to help them realize their dreams.

Accept and diligently carry out the commands of those in authority over you.

Skillful hands lead to productivity.

The world may be bad, but what can you do to make it better?

LIFE'S
LITTLE HANDBOOK
OF WISDOM

━━━━━━

Become quiet before God in the busiest
and noisiest part of your day.

Looking back on what God has done for
you strengthens your faith in the
future.

The way you deal with life each day
depends on what you bring to life each
day.

138

Leave your burdens at the feet of the Master and let Him bear them.

Worrying occurs when God is left out of the process.

If you find yourself putting your trust in money, intelligence, beauty, or success, remember that all these come from God. Think about where your trust really belongs.

▬▬▬

Stay in touch with family members. It's easy to ignore those closest to you.

There is a delicate balance between respecting your children's privacy and knowing what's going on in their lives.

Decorative magnets can display all kinds of stuff—but especially family pride—on your refrigerator door.

140

Provide your kids with a bulletin board
of their own so they can pin up personal
mementos.

Fly festive flags in front of your house.

Study the history of your town. Then
study its spiritual history. The future is
in your hands.

Living small does not mean sacrificing
integrity.

The manner in which you cultivate your
inner garden will be evident to all
manner of pests.

Become acquainted with classical
music.

If there's something in your closet you
haven't worn for years, give it to
someone who will wear it more often.

Next time one of your kids goes on a
youth retreat, volunteer to help before
you're called. (But ask your kids first.)

While the prosperous man often looks
over his shoulder with suspicion, one
experiencing adversity looks ahead with
hope.

Anything within the scope of your
responsibility will decay without
constant attention.

God does not help us because we deserve it; He helps us because He loves us.

Attend every open house at your children's schools.

Applaud younger children when they role play.

145

■■■■■■■

Teach older children how to role play.

If you seek wisdom over opportunity,
opportunity will usually follow.

Scaffolding must stay on the outside
until there's enough strength on the
inside to stand alone.

Fear is the prelude to hope.

Being misunderstood is not so bad.
Some of the world's greatest leaders
have been misunderstood at one time or
another.

People who talk a lot about themselves
seldom want to hear what others have
to say.

One quality of God's nature that should make us tremble is His justice.

When someone does something good for you, never forget it.

When you do something nice for someone else, let it go immediately.

When you give a gift, expect nothing in
return.

Deal with jealousy the moment it enters
your life. Otherwise fear will come
knocking.

If you skate on thin ice, make sure
you're going fast.

A person who fears being despised is probably despicable.

Money is like fertilizer: It's not much good unless it's spread around.

If you go through life without the Lord, this world will seem like a hospital, a place to get sick and die.

If you go through life with the Lord, this world will seem like an inn, a place to stay while you're passing through.

Prefer a prudent enemy to an indiscreet friend.

That which is great is not always worthy of praise, but that which is worthy of praise is always great.

■■■■■■

There are born leaders and there are leaders who are made. And then there are those who become leaders out of necessity.

Character is one of those qualities that is attained slowly.

The call of God is sometimes difficult to discern.

Once discerned, the call of God is
difficult to avoid.

A great biographer once said that the
history of the world is merely the
biography of great people.

Write an autobiography and update it
annually.

LIFE'S
LITTLE HANDBOOK
OF WISDOM

A truly eloquent speech includes all that
is necessary, and no more.

You begin to seek God for who He is
when you stop seeking Him for what He
can do for you.

Friendships are built gradually but can
be destroyed quickly.

Take responsibility for developing positive habits. You are accountable to your Heavenly Father.

You can't always control the kind of service you receive, but you can always control the kind of gratitude you deliver.

Sometimes the most effective words of comfort are no words at all.

∎

As you grow older, eat increasingly less
and infinitely better.

Fitness of the soul should take priority
over fitness of the body, but the two are
not necessarily mutually exclusive.

Live humbly and pray likewise.

Rising early to meet the Lord gives you a jump on the day. Meeting God at night enables you to reflect on the day. Either option is good.

The advantage of meeting God at the same time each day is that you don't have to decide when you are going to do it.

———

There is no such thing as a successful or unsuccessful prayer.

Hope is no stronger than the person in whom it is placed.

Develop a recreational activity your family can do together, and then enjoy it regularly.

Let your kids help you plan your next vacation.

Physical fitness should be a discipline, not an obsession.

Introduce your family to great works of art. Display prints of favorite paintings in your home.

People of God may not talk about their prayer life, but their lives speak volumes.

Even if you don't *feel* God is close to you, it is possible at the same time to *know* He is near.

At its core, prayer is giving yourself to God.

Character is no more a substitute for faith than morality is a substitute for holiness.

People of low ambition are overly critical because so much in life is beyond their reach.

Look for the best in others, but search yourself for flaws.

A man of integrity makes an easy
target for critics because he stands
upright.

An unprincipled woman is often ignored
because she cowers in the dark.

The person dependent on Christ has the
amazing ability to maintain a steady
ship on a stormy sea.

162

Resist the natural inclination to hold adversity at arm's length. Embrace it willingly.

There are those who experience joy and terror simultaneously. Ask a parent whose teenager has just obtained a driver's license.

True education must begin by instilling
in children a deep sense of honesty.

Building character into your kids helps
develop your own.

Enthusiasm breeds positive behavior.

Positive behavior produces credibility.

Circumstances may be outside our control, but the way we respond to them is not.

The insight of one person can become wisdom for many.

▬▬▬

Personal happiness is most easily
gained by bringing happiness to others.

While the poor dream of having riches,
the wealthy long for simplicity.

Great art brings the head and the heart
together.

Adversity produces heartache when it comes, and exhilaration when it goes.

If we want to see others fail, our successes are empty achievements.

Love first if you long to be loved.

■■■■■

Being deprived of something you desire
is better than having something you
despise.

Where it is impossible to create
something new, try to improve what is
already there.

When you think you've learned enough,
you haven't.

You will impress more people by
listening than talking.

The highest learning is to know God
and, from that knowledge, to love Him.

The ultimate human arrogance is when
a man thinks God exists because he
thought Him up.

▬▬▬

An active mind is like a truckstop:
always open.

Memory, like a muscle, needs to be
exercised daily.

All of us want to live long, but few want
to be old.

Joy comes from controlling, rather than exercising, your passions.

Get away with your spouse for one uninterrupted weekend a year.

Stand by your kids in good times and bad; pray for them unceasingly; love them unconditionally. Nothing is easier or harder.

171

Fight the natural tendency to talk
rather than listen to your kids.

Make your house the center of activity
in your neighborhood.

The surest way to gain a greater
appreciation for your hometown is to
live somewhere else for a while.

The first step on the path to
commitment is making up your mind.

Discover and study your spiritual gifts.
They are a source of energy.

Daily thank the Lord for His gifts.

ISBN 1-55748-644-1

9 781557 486448

90000